D1359433

HOW TO BE

POSITIVE

AND HAPPY

igloobooks

igloobooks

Written by Belinda Campbell
Designed by Dave Chapman
Edited by Bobby Newlyn-Jones

Copyright © 2019 Igloo Books Ltd

An imprint of Igloo Books Group,
part of Bonnier Books UK
bonnierbooks.co.uk

Published in 2019
by Igloo Books Ltd, Cottage Farm
Sywell, NN6 0BJ

Manufactured in China. 1119 001
10 9 8 7 6 5 4 3 2 1

Library of Congress Cataloging-in-Publication
Data is available upon request.

ISBN 978-1-83852-539-2
IglooBooks.com
bonnierbooks.co.uk

Introduction

Our mindful and positive selves can sometimes get a little lost among the noise and stress of our modern day lives. If setting an early alarm for that morning spin class is just not happening, then use this dip-in guide to find those uplifting moments of positivity during your busy day.

This book doesn't ask you to sign up for anything, and no prior experience or expensive gym membership is required. Whenever you need a moment of brightness on a dull day, simply open this book at random and find a page which is right for you, then revisit the activities which you find work best. There are loads to choose from, whether you just need an inspiring phrase or a reflective writing activity.

Kick-start your day with a confident affirmation, treat yourself to a tea break meditation, or close your day with an empowering breathing practice, and feel the positivity ease back into your life and self.

GOOD MORNING AFFIRMATIONS

POSITIVE AFFIRMATIONS ARE A PERFECT WAY TO BOOST YOUR DAY. BUT WHAT ARE THEY EXACTLY?

SIMPLY PUT, AFFIRMATIONS ARE MANTRAS OR POSITIVE STATEMENTS OF TRUTH ABOUT WHO YOU WANT TO BE. TRY A FEW OF THE BELOW TO GET YOU STARTED:

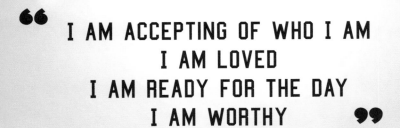

> **I AM ACCEPTING OF WHO I AM**
> **I AM LOVED**
> **I AM READY FOR THE DAY**
> **I AM WORTHY**

ALWAYS SPOKEN IN THE PRESENT TENSE, MANTRAS ARE A POSITIVE WAY TO STEP INTO THE MINDFUL PRESENT. TRY AND MAKE YOUR OWN PERSONAL MANTRAS TO BEST SUIT YOUR NEEDS.

SUNSHINE BREATH

Our emotions can be as unpredictable as the weather, but this breathing exercise can try and shine a light on those darker days.

Find a relaxed position, sitting or lying down, and close your eyes.

Draw your focus to your breathing. Feel each breath go in and each breath leave.

When you next breathe in, imagine your breath is a golden wash of sunshine flooding your body with warmth. When you breathe out, see any darkness lingering inside you leave with your breath.

Repeat until there is nothing but light inside of you.

Embrace your
Nature

What if you accepted everything about yourself today? Self-improvement can be a positive thing, but it can also lead to feeling like we constantly need to be better than who we currently are.

Look at nature, the sunflower doesn't try and be a rose, a robin doesn't try to be an eagle. Today, accept your own nature and see how you feel by the end of the day.

Breathe Victorious

The Ujjayi Breath, a yoga breathing technique that is commonly translated as the 'victorious breath,' is wonderful at giving you that winning attitude to start your day!

Ensure that you're sitting comfortably, then roll your shoulders up and back. Start to deepen your breath, inhaling through the nose and exhaling with a soft audible 'haah' through your mouth — as if you're misting up a window pane or mirror with your breath.

Feel a slight tightening in the back of your throat which transforms your breath into the soothing sound of the ocean.

When you are comfortable with this gentle tightening in the back of the throat, close your mouth and continue the exercise by breathing in through the nose, and out through the nose.

Try to continue making the soft 'haah' sound with your mouth now closed. Stay mindful to the sound of your breath and tap into a more triumphant you.

Let your
darker days
make your
better days
shine even
brighter.

Flattery will get you everywhere

It's easy to stress about the things we do not like about ourselves, but rarely do we try to think about what we love about ourselves. Whether you like the sound of your name or your choice in books, compile a list of things that you love and appreciate about yourself.

-
-
-
-
-
-

Keep this list safe and read it over when you need a positive reminder of all the good things that you bring to the world. As you grow, so should this list, so keep adding to it.

CONFIDENT YOU

As we are always growing and changing, our confidence in ourselves does too. Write three things that you have learned about yourself lately, trying to keep them as neutral facts such as 'I don't like sprouts,' 'I can name all the band members in Destiny's Child,' 'I enjoy writing poems,' or 'I can't touch my toes.'

Now, look at all the things you have found out about yourself recently. Do not attach judgment to them. See yourself for you and your confidence will grow as your self-assurance does.

CLEAR-HEADED COMMUTE

Whether you walk the whole way to work or just the last 60 seconds to your office door or desk, you can practice this meditation to wake a more positive, present you.

As you start your walk, pay attention to each step you take: the sounds, the touch, the speed. Keep an even and slow pace to match comfortably with your breathing.

Always take notice of your surroundings and see how everything is connected. Your feet to your shoes, your shoes to the pavement, the pavement to the trees, the trees to the birds, the birds to the air.

If you have walked this route many times, avoid switching on your autopilot as you tread the same old steps. Continue to stay present, notice what is new: the sounds, the weather, the color of the cars parked nearby.

Practice this positive focus before you begin work and see how it boosts your productivity.

Find Your Half-smile

If you look at images of the happy Buddha, you'll often see him with a peaceful half-smile on his face; this smile can symbolize a joy in the present and a total lack of ego.

When you find yourself in moments that are lacking joy or perhaps full of ego, standing in a queue or in a work meeting, try to adopt a half-smile. As you breathe in, feel the corners of your mouth lift ever so slightly. Hold this half-smile for a few breaths as you relax into your positive present.

Give it a go.

YOU ARE THE SPEAKER AND THE LISTENER TO YOUR OWN internal VOICE.

DECIDE WHAT YOU WANT TO SAY AND HEAR.

Fall in love with yourself and make your own mixtape of all your favorite songs which make you feel happy and positive. It could be in the form of a playlist, CD, or even an actual cassette tape!

Once you have your self-love songs ready, pick out your favorite lyrics. Keep these words near you in a small notebook, hang them above your head in a frame, or hum them to yourself morning and night. This way, you're instantly ready to remind yourself that you are always loved and that you have great taste in music!

dream
out
loud

Don't be afraid of vocalizing what you want and chasing your dreams. If you're not ready to share your hopes for the future with your friends and family just yet, start by sharing them wholeheartedly with yourself. Allow yourself to imagine reaching your dreams, visualize how it will feel when you do.

Hold onto this feeling as you go about your daily life, but also tap into it in private moments to intensify your positive drive.

Sweet Silence

If you don't have anything nice to say...

Most of us are taught this trick of silence when we are young, but our inner negative voice wasn't always taught the same manners. Imagine yourself as a parent and your whining voice of self-doubt is a child. As soon as it begins talking rudely or out of turn, remind them that if they do not have anything positive to say then they should not say anything at all.

Be patient and persistent with this practice (just as you would with a child) and restore sweet silence to your mind.

POST SOME POSITIVITY

Think of how great it is to receive something through the post that isn't just your phone bill or junk mail.

Share that joy by writing a thank you card to someone you think deserves some positive post. It will have the double positive effect of not only reminding you of someone you are grateful to have in your life, but it will also make them feel great about themselves too.

WIN WIN.

I'Mpossible

Write a list of all the impossible things you have done in your life – anything that at one time you felt was near-impossible, but you persevered and came up tops. These may be big or small, from getting out of bed in the morning to skydiving! Fill in the sentences below and look back over all the things that you made possible:

I never thought I would_____but I did.

Younger me would never have_____but I did.

Now think of future-you looking back on today-you. What feels impossible today that future you will accomplish?

I could never_____... but future me will!

POSITIVE PRIDE

WHEN YOU NEED A BOOST OF SELF-CONFIDENCE, GIVE THIS PLAYFUL 'LION'S BREATH' EXERCISE A GO.

Start by sitting with your legs crossed or folded beneath you with your buttocks resting on your heels. Loop your shoulders up and over towards your back, releasing any tension and creating an open space between the ears and the shoulders. Inhale through the nose and exhale with a hissing 'haaaaah' sound through the mouth. Inhale again and as you breathe out, take your gaze upwards and stick your tongue out and down.

Take five of these lion breaths and be mindful to not hold any tension in your jaw, neck, and shoulders as you repeat. Notice at the end of this exercise how your mind and body feel confident to take the day.

Write a WRONG

Do you cringe when you think of your past mistakes? Do your last week's antics fill you with dread?

Whether it's to yesterday's you or last year's you, choose a younger you to write a letter to. Start by forgiving them for whatever it is that you have been holding on to. Continue the letter by thanking them for getting you this far in your life. Tell them all the good things they can look forward to in their life.

Finish your letter by thanking them for all the things that you are and for all that you have.

Write your letter here:

"I don't know what I'm doing"

Said everyone, everywhere!

FUEL YOUR FULFILLMENT

In our busy lives, a healthy diet can fall right to the bottom of our priorities. Whether you are feeling great or not, check in with yourself regularly to make sure you are giving your body what it needs.

Ask yourself, when was the last time I ate something nutritious? Do I need a glass of water?

Think of yourself as an attentive waiter and keep asking yourself if you need anything - give yourself a generous tip at the end of the day if you have been extra attentive!

FRAME YOUR DAY YOUR WAY

Positive affirmations are brilliant at boosting your self-belief. Incorporating them into your breathing exercises can help you focus on actualizing your aims.

Try to insert this one into your morning routine to help your day be framed in positivity. Take a deep breath in and then out. As you breathe in, think 'Today is full of opportunity,' and when you breathe out continue with 'and I am open to it all.' Repeat in nice, long, even breaths up to ten times.

WASH AWAY THE DAY

Imagine an empty washbasin with a stopper placed in the bottom. There are two faucets over the basin. One is your 'positive faucet' and the other is your 'negative faucet.' Think about your day from start to finish. How much of it was filled with positive energy and how much was filled with negative?

Now, turn each faucet to fill your sink up with how your day went. Look at the waters coming from each faucet at their different strengths and speeds. Notice how the water from both faucets is clear and cool. Ask yourself, what is the difference between these two faucets aside from their names? When the washbasin is full, remove the stopper and see your day circle and disappear.

Practice this one at the end of a day to reflect and let go of any negative energy.

JOIN THE
CIRCUS

When you want to run away from the scary reality of life, running off to join the circus may have crossed your mind!

For days like these, try visualizing yourself as an expert tightrope walker. Notice how your presence commands silence from your audience. Begin to walk the rope slowly and confidently.

Once you have finished walking and have absorbed all the applause, finish the exercise with a triumphant breath.

As you work through your tasks today, channel your courageous tightrope walker and find that the negative fears that you had for the day ahead no longer seem so scary.

Try to change what you can and learn to love what you can't.

Feel Better
in Five

Fill in the five feel-good blanks below
for a quick boost of positivity.

I love_____ about myself

I love the way I _____

I am happy with _____

I love my _____

_____ makes me happy

Come back to this page whenever you need a reminder.
Why not add some more?

Inhalation Inspiration

Discover the full potential of your breath by experimenting with this 1:2:1 ratio breathing exercise. The principle is that you inhale for the count of one, exhale for two, pause for one. When it comes to pausing, don't make this an emergency stop, think of it as approaching the top of a hill before rolling down the other side of it.

Once you've wrapped your head around the 1:2:1, experiment with the ratios and find what suits you. Maybe breathe in for the count of two, exhale for four, pause for two. Or inhale for three, exhale for six, pause for three.

Practice whatever fills you with the greatest sense of positive focus.

DEFEAT
THE
DEFEATIST

Don't take your thoughts as facts. Sometimes our inner naysaying voices can shout their downer opinions to you as if they were gospel.

One way to quieten those negative thoughts is to question their validity. If you were a journalist, you would always check your sources before printing them as facts - do the same for your inner voice before letting them publish your story for you. Ask yourself, where has that thought come from? Is there any evidence to back up that thought? Would others support this viewpoint? What's the other side of this story?

Find that there is always another, more positive side and explore it further.

Bec**OM**e positive

The ancient and sacred Hindu symbol of Aum, familiarly known and heard as Om, is a powerfully rich sound that can be chanted in yoga classes, meditation or as part of a breathing practice.

Begin by sitting upright in a chair or on the floor with your legs crossed. Breathe in through your nose and open your mouth as you begin to sound your first 'om.' Close your mouth as you continue the sound.

Notice the vibration cleansing through your body. If you start to feel a bit silly, embrace it! It's normal to feel out of your comfort zone for this one, try to enjoy it!

FIND A
SOLUTION

Sometimes, an answer may feel as if it's on the tip of your tongue, but the more you chase it, the further it runs away from you. Instead of becoming disheartened or frustrated by this feeling, try to embrace the mental blankness.

Close your eyes, take your mind to your breathing, and soften your gaze so that you are focused on nothing in particular. Empty your mind of the problem you're facing. Let thoughts pass through. Don't hold onto to any of them, just let them keep moving; think of your thoughts as birds flying across the sky.

Practice this meditation daily for a week and see if any of these twittering thoughts turn into possible solutions.

Good Mood Board

Whether it's on your computer or craft table, making a mood board can allow you to identify and focus on your dreams for the future.

Make yours and include inspirational quotes, people who motivate you, or colors that excite you. Keep adding to your board and store it somewhere where you can access it regularly.

Reminding yourself of your aims will encourage you to work at them and increase your chances of achieving them!

EAT DRINK AND BE POSITIVE

Make every day a celebration dinner, whether you're eating grilled cheese or a steak dinner!

The evening meal marks the end of another day in your life. Whether you have thrived or simply survived, today is another day that you have somehow contributed to or learned something from.

So, make your dinner time a moment to celebrate another day done!

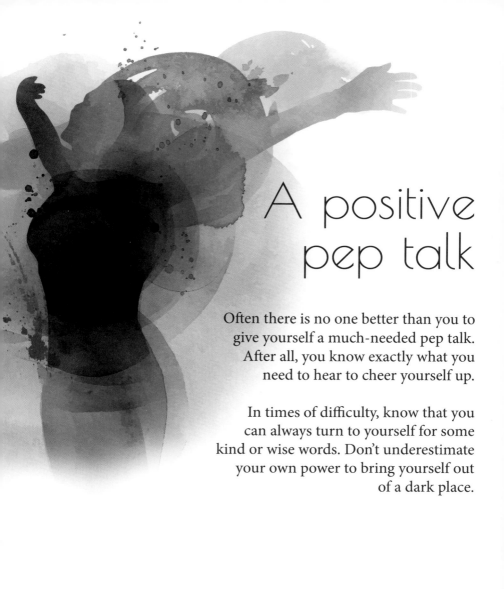

A positive pep talk

Often there is no one better than you to give yourself a much-needed pep talk. After all, you know exactly what you need to hear to cheer yourself up.

In times of difficulty, know that you can always turn to yourself for some kind or wise words. Don't underestimate your own power to bring yourself out of a dark place.

A
MISTAKE
— is just a —
MEMORABLE
LESSON IF YOU

CAN
LEARN
something
FROM
IT

I WOKE UP LIKE THIS

Some days you wake up in a terrible mood,
but how do you get out of it?

Start by accepting how you are feeling today.
Being mindful is not about resisting your racing mind and
negative thoughts, it is about acknowledging them for what
they are and letting them run their course. As soon as you
stop fighting your feelings, you'll immediately feel happier
and have more energy to get on with the rest of your day.

Begin a better day by being at peace with how
you are feeling at this moment.

Tune into you

Begin by checking in with your head, neck, and shoulders, and letting go of any tension.

Take a nice long breath in through your nose and – before you exhale through your mouth – purse your lips ready to whistle. Tune in to the sound of your whistling. Find the joy in it and feel its invigorating effects. Repeat as before or try whistling on your inhale and exhale for a few breaths.

Not a whistler? Not a problem. This may be even more of a mindful exercise for you as your concentration on the act of whistling will be increased!

Speak to
yourself with
love only.

Smile

While we think of smiling being a product of our happiness, what's to stop ourselves from switching this around and smiling to encourage some happiness?

Smiling helps our facial muscles relax and is thought to improve our relationships, invite success, and even boost your immune system (thanks to its powers of relaxation).

If you're worried about looking like a Cheshire cat, opt for a more demure Mona Lisa or Buddha half-smile. Make a smile the last thing you put on before leaving your door and see where the day takes you!

Find your HAPPY

Write a list of things that you enjoy doing most. It might include:

- Yoga
- Eating brunch
- Going to the cinema
- Reading
- Playing sports
- Walking the dog

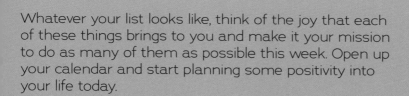

Whatever your list looks like, think of the joy that each of these things brings to you and make it your mission to do as many of them as possible this week. Open up your calendar and start planning some positivity into your life today.

Write your list here:

....

....

....

....

....

....

....

....

....

....

Take a breather

Sit up nice and tall to allow yourself to take full, invigorating breaths. Try to make your breaths in and out the same length.

When you are ready, begin to deepen your breath to a 1:2 ratio – breathing in for the count of two and out for four, or in for three and out for six. Essentially, your breaths out should be twice as long as your breaths in.

Be careful not to stretch yourself and turn into a gasping fish! As with any breath, make it smooth and be mindful of what feels good to you. Practice for five minutes and find yourself prepared for whatever the day has in store for you.

THE ARCHER'S BREATH

In archery, many instructors will encourage you to take a deep breath before you release your arrow to maximize your chances of hitting your target.

For this breathing exercise, channel your inner archer and, as you inhale, imagine your target is in clear sight. Before you release your arrow of intent, exhale your breath with calm control.

Try taking this breath when you have clear intentions that you need to achieve and want to be filled with a positive focus.

Bee positive

For when you need some feel-good vibrations,
try the yoga breathing technique, Bhramari,
also known as the 'humming bee breath.'

Ready yourself by taking a few deep
cleansing breaths. Relax your forehead,
your jawline, your neck, and your shoulders.

As with any breathing exercise, do what
feels comfortable and never force your
breath or body beyond its personal capability.
Inhale through your nose, keeping your mouth
gently closed. Exhale through your nose
and begin to make a gentle humming sound.

Cover your ears softly with the tips of your
index fingers (do not put your fingers inside
your ear). Inhale through the nose and repeat
as before, feeling the positive vibrations
travel through you.

ACTIVATE YOUR HAPPY

Exercise can have hugely positive effects on our moods, boosting circulation and producing those feel-good endorphins. Think about ways in which you can make some small changes to your everyday life to increase your daily activity.

It may be walking to work instead of driving, taking stairs over elevators, or doing your grocery shop in-store rather than getting food delivered. Everyone's physical capabilities are unique to them, so always check with your doctor before making any big changes to your routines.

Try making just one active change in your daily life and see how it affects your mood. Use the space on the opposite page to record these little changes and how they made you feel.

Activity

....
....
....
....
....
....
....
....
....
....
....
....
....
....
....
....
....

I felt...

....
....
....
....
....
....
....
....
....
....
....
....
....
....
....
....
....

Looking in the mirror can be an uncomfortable thing to do for a lot of people, but it can also help us reflect on the attitudes that we have towards ourselves, inside and out.

Place yourself in front of a mirror. What are the first things you notice about yourself? Close your eyes for one deep breath. When you open your eyes again, see yourself through the eyes of someone who cares for you. What are the first things they see about you? Close your eyes for another deep breath and when you open them next, look through your own eyes again but with the kindness of a loved one.

What new things can you see through this change of gaze? Try to include attributes which are not reflected in the mirror like your intelligence, your humor, your talents at karaoke etc.

Practice this exercise regularly so that this positive gaze becomes second nature.

ACCEPT ADMIRATION

Sometimes, as bizarre as it sounds, it is hard to hear someone say nice things about ourselves. Having someone notice our hair, clothes, work, or other means that people see you, can leave us feeling self-conscious and wanting to hide.

Make a promise to yourself that the next time someone compliments you, you will take it with open arms and thank them. It will leave them and you feeling happier and confident.

Social
Spring Clean

This one is for the technoholics! Take a look at the accounts that you are following on your most used social media platforms. Be mindful of how these images or words make you feel. If there are some that make you feel bad in any way, unfollow or silence their notifications so they are no longer coming up on your feed. For the people that inspire positivity in you, keep following them and see if there are any other similar accounts that you could follow for more feel-good vibes!

FIND YOUR

RHYTHM

Find a piece of music that brings you joy and happiness. It can be any genre and any pace, all that's important is the positive feeling it fills you with.

Sitting comfortably, take your attention to your breath. Try to feel the rhythm in your breath in the music that is playing. Do not change your breathing to match the music. Instead, see how your breath and the music can coexist. When the sounds of your chosen song fill the air, think of your breath sharing that same air. As the music finishes, close your practice with a final deep breath.

Carry this song and your uplifting connection with it throughout your day.

Let loose

Meditation is all about observing, so let your mind run freely like a rebellious toddler for two minutes. Notice where it goes? What do your thoughts look like?

Do it again for another two minutes. Get to know how your thoughts work and what they look like in this present moment. Are they erratic? Numerous? Contradictory? Confused?

Focus on your unfocused state for as long as you can, and enjoy finding out what positive things you can learn from letting your mind run loose for a while.

The Perfect Plus One

To wake up feeling
refreshed and ready
for a positive start
to your day, try this
breathing exercise
before bed.

Take a few deep breaths
before you begin. When you
next breathe in, begin
counting in your mind. As
you reach the end of your
inhalation, add one to the
number you reached and make
that your target length for
your exhalation. So, if your
inward breath was three seconds
long, try to make breathing out
last for four seconds.

Continue this exercise until you
can feel your breath deepen after
a while, but try to continue breathing
deeply as you fall into a peaceful sleep.

Finding your true worth is the richest you will ever be.

If you have a target that you are trying to realize but negativity is getting in the way of making it feel possible, try this visualization exercise.

In an upright seated or lying down position, straighten the length of your spine. Feel the satisfying weight of a medal hanging around your neck. Imagine the color of the ribbon, the thickness of the material attached to the heavy metal resting on your chest.

Take the cool metal in your hand and move your hand up and down, feeling its weight. Notice that the medal has some text written into it. Read what the text says. Remember how reading these words made you feel.

Try this one any time you need to channel a winning attitude!

A sigh of thanks

Tap your breathing into the gifts of the day.

Prepare yourself by taking a few regular breaths. When you next breathe in, identify something you are grateful for and give a mindful thanks to it as you breathe out.

For example, inhale 'hello sunny day' and sigh out 'thank you sunny day.' Inhale 'hello working legs,' sigh out 'thank you working legs.' Inhale 'hello dogs of the world,' sigh out 'thank you dogs of the world.'

Tap into this grateful breath to invite a more positive attitude.

POWER POSING

Think of your favorite superheroes standing strong and fearless in the face of adversity! Chances are you have imagined them in their signature 'power poses.' Wonder Woman with her hands on her hips, Superman with his arms outstretched flying.

With no tight-fitting clothing needed, find a space where you have plenty of room to stretch your arms and legs out. Once you have your space, try to adopt either a familiar superhero power pose or make one up of your own. Find the confidence to fill the space and see how changing your posture can affect your mood.

See your

Best
You

See yourself in a more positive light with this written exercise.

On this side of the line, write all the not-so-nice words that you think have been or have heard used to describe you.

Now on the right side (in more ways than one), write down the positive ways to look at those negatives, e.g.: Ugly - Unique Pushover - Generous

The first few may be tricky, but this is something that will become easier over time with regular practice.

LEARN LIKE A PRO

After experiencing a challenging relationship, meeting, day, or even year, sometimes all we can see are the negatives attached to those experiences. Did we even pause to consider the pros that could be taken away from these challenges?

WRITE DOWN THREE THINGS THAT YOU LEARNED FROM YOUR LAST CHALLENGING EXPERIENCE.

1.

2.

3.

Read them back, let them be your focus when you look at those memories. Learning is always a positive, it's how we grow and become more compassionate individuals, so learn like a pro and lose the cons by practicing this exercise weekly.

Try your best

and let others do their worst!

A breath
of fresh air

We always keep a little oxygen in our lungs, but by gently encouraging more breath to leave our lungs we can take bigger, brand new breaths of oxygen.

Begin by checking in with your head, neck, and shoulders, and try to let go of any tension that you might be holding onto in those areas. Take a few easy breaths. Notice how deep or shallow your breathing is right now. Take a deep breath in and then out.

As you reach the end of breathing out, imagine that you need to gently cough and see if there is any more breath that you can expel before you next breathe in. On your next intake of breath, enjoy the buoyant feeling of being able to take in even more delicious oxygen.

Repeat two or three times and see how you feel. Take care not to cause your body any discomfort. Breathing should always be a rejuvenating and soothing practice.

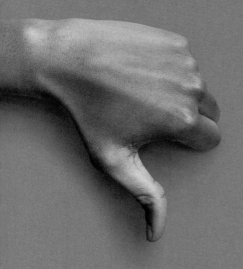

'No'

IS NOT A
NEGATIVE.

Dress in Success

Getting dressed every morning
is part of most people's lives,
so why not boost this everyday
practice with some
positive thinking?

The aim of the game is simple,
for each item you put on, put
on a piece of positivity that will
assist you through your day. As you
put on your socks, put on gratitude.
As you put on a t-shirt, put on courage.
As you zip up your coat, surround yourself
with self-acceptance. Soon you will be
dressed for anything coming your way!

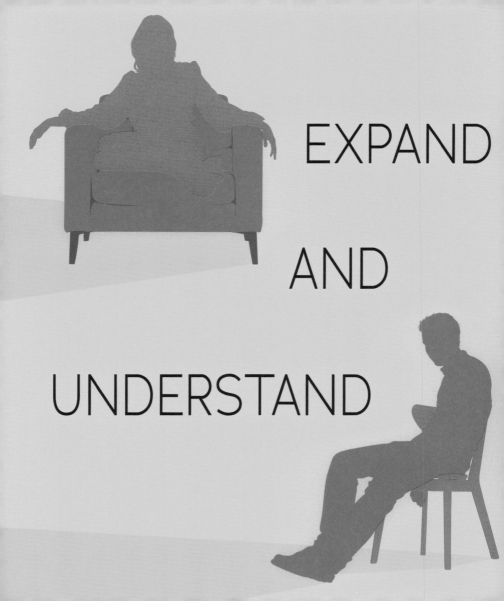

EXPAND

AND

UNDERSTAND

A positive way to transform your negativity is to turn it into compassion by expanding your understanding.

Find a comfortable seated position and take three deep breaths. Let your mind travel to a negative interaction you had recently, whether that was online, in person, or over the phone.

Rather than remembering the situation from your perspective, try to imagine it from the other person's end. If there were several people involved, spend a little time in each of their shoes. Approach the situation from all angles.

Keep taking deep breaths as you try to expand your understanding and release any negativity.

GIVE YOUR FEARS THE
'WHAT IF'!

Every time self-doubt starts to creep its
way in, give it the 'what if' treatment.

- **I'M NOT WORKING FAST ENOUGH. WHAT IF I GAVE MYSELF MORE TIME?**

- **I'M NOT AS GOOD AS THAT PERSON. WHAT IF I STOPPED COMPARING MYSELF TO OTHERS?**

- **I'M GOING TO FAIL. WHAT IF I SUCCEED?**

- **WHAT IF THEY SAY NO? WHAT IF THEY SAY YES?!**

-

-

-

This is a great way to start problem-solving
and find a positive solution.

Comparing with one another leads to competition, supporting one another leads to winning.

Soar above it all and enjoy the view

PLAN YOUR HAPPINESS

All the best intentions can be abandoned when we don't devote the time to make them happen.

Go grab your calendar or open the one on your phone. Choose a time of day that you want to give yourself a boost of positivity and at that time each day for the next week, write 'pick up this book.'

Even if you only give yourself a five-minute slot, choose a regular moment in your day that you can take for yourself. Keep it up for a week and start to feel the uplifting benefits of taking time for yourself.

Rewrite your story

Take yourself to a quiet spot somewhere or, if that isn't available to you, try to tune into just one sound that you can hear currently – maybe some talking or nearby music. Take a moment to check in with your breath.

Now close your eyes and imagine your mind is a blank dry-erase board. There are marker pens to one side and an eraser on the other. Singular words or sentences begin to appear on the board. Read them and ask yourself how they make you feel. If the answer is good then keep the writing on the board, if the answer is bad then reach for the eraser and wipe the board clean. Pick up one of the pens and take the power of writing your personal story into your own hands; it's your story after all.

Try this exercise when you need to make a positive change and take charge of your life.

ENCOURAGE YOUR COURAGE

WRITE A LIST OF ALL THE COURAGEOUS THINGS YOU HAVE DONE IN YOUR LIFE. IT MAY BE SPEAKING IN PUBLIC, TRAVELING TO A NEW COUNTRY, OR STARTING A NEW JOB — HOWEVER BIG OR SMALL, WRITE THEM ALL DOWN. YOU DON'T HAVE TO BE SAVING LIVES TO FEEL THE POSITIVE RUSH OF TAKING A RISK NOW AND AGAIN. WHETHER YOUR RISKS PAID OFF IS NOT THE POINT OF THIS EXERCISE, IT IS ACKNOWLEDGING THE COURAGE THAT EACH OF THESE ACTIONS TOOK TO TRY. COURAGE IS CONTAGIOUS, SO ENCOURAGE MORE OF IT BY DOING THIS EXERCISE REGULARLY.

WONDERFUL WANDER

Begin your day by taking an early morning walk.
Before you flick to another page in this book
for fear of setting a 5 am alarm, ´early´ is
different for everyone so don´t let
this word scare you off!

Even if it is setting your alarm 15 minutes
earlier than normal to take a five-minute
or ten-minute stroll, the positive benefits
of doing so can still be felt. Whether it´s
a lap of the block or getting off the bus
a stop or two earlier, taking a walk can
boost your energy levels and allow
your mind a moment of energized
focus to start your day right.

The mindful drinking game!

Sometimes the trick to staying positive is remembering to take the time to adjust your negative outlook. Try this exercise if you're struggling to remember to dedicate time in your life to finding the positive.

Each time you take a drink, whether that's coffee, water, or juice, imagine you are going to make a toast of thanks to someone or something in your life. The toast can be a short and sweet 'Thanks for dogs!' or it could be something longer if you prefer. Make a gratitude list and refer back to it, or have a day of celebrating all things you.

The magic of
MANTRAS

Usually a single word or sound that you repeat, reciting mantras can have similar positive effects to affirmations but are more bite-size! Think of something that you would like to channel today and make it your mantra. It may be 'self-love,' 'confidence,' 'positivity,' or 'patience.' Try and keep it to one or two words to make it easy to remember and repeat.

Think of your chosen mantra throughout your day to tap into its positive meditative powers. Repeat it as you walk to work, turn on your computer, or as you focus on your breathing. Make it the background beat to everything you do to help invoke a mental clarity and positive state of mind.

TWIG YOUR TRIGGERS

Take a quiet moment to yourself, make a cup of tea or a hot water bottle. Get yourself comfortable and create a safe space. When you feel ready, begin writing down the names of things or people that trigger you in some way and your emotional response. Try filling in the below to get you started:

When I see images of _____ it makes me feel_____

When I speak to_____ it makes me feel_____

When I hear_____it makes me feel_____

_____

_____

_____

By being aware of what triggers certain emotions, you can feel better prepared and avoid certain negative triggers.

Positively Boring

Meditation does not have to be all eyes closed and legs crossed, we can find meditative moments in our everyday tasks – in fact, sometimes the most boring of chores are the most perfect times to treat our minds to a moment of the present.

When you're next making the bed or washing the car, instead of allowing your mind to drift off, focus on your task at hand. Mentally note the smells, sounds, touch, and taste attached to that chore. Tune into each of your senses one by one as you turn this dull moment into a positive, mindful one.

The Myth of 'Too'

Ever felt you were too this or too that? Or been told by someone else that you are too much of something or other?

In the left-hand column, write down all the things you believe you are too much of.

Now, in the right-hand column, remove the 'too's and find the positive truths hidden in these statements.

Too quiet – I am quiet

Too loud – I am loud

Too emotional – I am emotional

See how these things cease to be negative when you remove the myth of 'too'!

I'm too...

....

....

....

....

....

....

....

....

....

....

....

....

....

....

....

....

I am...

....

....

....

....

....

....

....

....

....

....

....

....

....

....

....

....

SHINE A POSITIVE LIGHT

Most of us have a few negative niggles that chant merrily away in our heads. Write down the negative voices you hear most often. They might be, 'I don't earn enough money,' 'I always say the wrong thing,' or 'I'm a bad friend.' Record a few below:

....

....

....

....

Now, rewrite each of these fears in a more positive light. They might change to, 'I'm going to find out how to increase my finances,' 'I will speak mindfully as I do openly,' or 'I will be a better friend than I have been recently.'

LET THESE NEW VOICES LEAD THE WAY

Roll with
the good days,

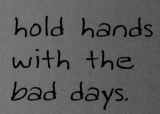

hold hands
with the
bad days.

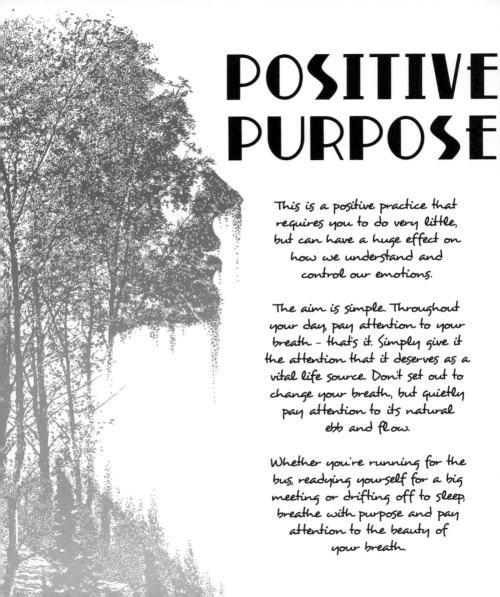

POSITIVE PURPOSE

This is a positive practice that requires you to do very little, but can have a huge effect on how we understand and control our emotions.

The aim is simple. Throughout your day, pay attention to your breath - that's it. Simply give it the attention that it deserves as a vital life source. Don't set out to change your breath, but quietly pay attention to its natural ebb and flow.

Whether you're running for the bus, readying yourself for a big meeting or drifting off to sleep, breathe with purpose and pay attention to the beauty of your breath.

BE
BALANCED

Staying positive is about accepting the good days with the bad and finding a balance that works for you. Sama Vritti - or 'Equal Breathing' - can help you find and accept that balance.

Take one deep breath before you begin your counting. When you next breathe in, begin counting in your head. Now, try to breathe out for the same length. So, if you breathed in for three seconds, breathe out for three seconds.

Don't be afraid to take your time with this one, you may not find the balance straight away. Don't force your breath - let your body ease into a slow and steady rhythm that works for you.

Think
of yourself as
the sun - rise and
you will
shine!

Your cheering champ

You don't have to be good at sports for this one, all you need is a willingness to hear nice things about yourself, which at times can be a real challenge.

If you need a positive boost, give this exercise a go. Every time you do something well, pretend you've scored in your favorite sport and give yourself an inner cheer. That coffee I made was great - woohoo! That email I wrote was really useful - awesome! Walking to the store just now saved me money and the environment

GO TEAM!

Carry this supportive voice with you throughout your day today.

Body

Scan

Checking in with your body makes you more aware of your needs and able to make the positive changes required.

Begin by lying down. Take a moment to get rested. Notice the parts of your body that are making contact with the surface that you are lying on, be it a bed, grass, or carpet.

Take your awareness to your breathing and enjoy a couple of regular breaths or perhaps some belly breaths. Starting at the tips of your toes, begin mentally scanning your body. Notice how every part of you is feeling today.

What are your energy levels like? Are you tired? Is your foot itchy? Are you thirsty? Do you have a headache?

Continue the scan through legs, arms, torso, face, until you have checked in with your entire self. When you listen to your body it can often tell you what it needs, so do a regular body scan to listen out for what your body is trying to tell you.

BE THE LOVE
THAT YOU ARE
LOOKING FOR

Belly Breathing

Practice your belly (or abdominal) breathing to maximize the positive effects of deep breathing.

Find a comfortable place to sit or lie down. Place a hand on your stomach, just below your navel. Once you are comfy, take a nice long breath in through your nose and feel the air traveling all the way down into your belly. Feel your hand rise gently as your abdomen expands with the fresh oxygen.

Breathe out through your mouth and repeat. Focus on the slow but powerful rise and fall of your hand. Try to breathe deeply into the belly every day to keep yourself happy and healthy.

The Gratitude
Attitude

There's nothing quite as effective at lifting yourself out of a dark place as listing all the wonderful things in your life that you are grateful for.

With the hopes of filling every page one day, find a notebook in which you want to begin writing all the things that you are grateful for.

Whether they are big or small things, people or places, write down everything that helps bring a smile to your face.

Keep this book somewhere where you can reach for it regularly so you can read and write down all the best bits of life!

To-try-list

A to-do-list can sometimes just be a visual reminder of all the things that we have failed to do that day and be a bit of a buzzkill to our positivity levels. If you need a boost of positive energy when it comes to increasing your productivity, why not write yourself a 'to-try-list' instead?

- Try to be on my phone less
- Try to make my lunches this week
- Try to meet someone new
-
-
-
-
-
-

Plan Your **Perfect Day**

Imagination is a powerful tool that can bring our moods up and down. Imagining all the things that could go wrong in our day can be unnecessarily exhausting on our bodies and spirit. If you are in the habit of thinking the worst, then this meditation is for you.

In your mind, go through the activities of the day ahead. Think about the ways in which each one could go well from start to finish. Imagine what you want to get out of the day and home in on that optimistic approach.

Close your practice with a deep breath. Realize that your plan for today hasn't changed, but your attitude towards it has!

ACHIEVE YOUR AMBITIONS

While learning to dance, speak a new language, or play the guitar are all brilliant ambitions, beginning a big task like these can feel really daunting! Begin by taking your main objective and start to break it down.

If you want to learn a new language, for example, write down individual action points, like below:

- Sign up to a beginner's class
- Download a language app
- Ask colleagues, friends, or family if anyone speaks that language already
- Practice for ten minutes every day

Break down your aims and get closer to achieving them with every step!

Be a DOG

Not walking around on all-fours or licking people's faces! Try being a dog in the sense of channeling their endless joy and enthusiasm for life.

Imagine a dog and see how the simplest of things bring them excitement: food, a walk, spending time with loved ones. Choose now to enjoy one, two, or all three of these basic pleasures and stay present as you experience each one just as a dog would.

Try living your whole day like a dog and find the clear joy of loving each present moment.

Welcome the world

Negativity can sometimes manifest itself as resistance. If we don't feel good about something, we don't want to do it! Especially if it's unknown territory.

In an upright seated position, sit up tall with your chest open and your face ever so slightly tilted upward. Empty your mind of what you think your day might look like and recite to yourself, 'I welcome whatever the day has in store for me.' Breathe in deeply and repeat this affirmation as you breathe out.

Start your day with this welcome meditation and see if you can approach your day with less resistance.

TURN YOUR POTHOLES INTO POSITIVES

'Failure' is part of everyone's life. Things don't always work out how we thought they would, so we stamp them with a big 'FAILED' sign.

Look back on all the times in your life that have felt like your endeavours have fallen short.

Keep these memories in your head and write down one thing you learnt from each one. Think about how you are a more experienced and compassionate person from having learnt each of these things.

Hold onto this feeling of achievement and the focus on failing will begin to fade.

MEMORIES

I LEARNED

STRIP OFF THE NEGATIVITY

Just as you can dress yourself in success,
you can pick up negativity throughout your day
and be heavily weighed down with it by night time.
As you undress for bed, with each item of clothing you
take off, remove one of the negative thoughts that
you have been carrying with you.

As your socks and pants go in the dirty laundry, so do your
self-doubt and fears. Revel in this lighter you for a moment
and find yourself ready for a positive rest.

POSITIVE PARTY

After a difficult day, sometimes a party is in order. Sit in an active position, with your back nice and tall. Place your hands on your knees and keep your face lifted slightly upwards. Relax, but avoid slouching.

Now, imagine there is a room full of your favorite friends, family members, book characters, even celebrities – this is your party, the invite list is totally up to you! Each person you meet at this party stops and says something nice to you.

Bask in this positive party for a little while and when you are ready to leave, express your gratitude and thank everyone for coming before you make your exit.

THE GET UP AND GO SHOW

Asking questions is the best way to get to know someone better, but we don't often try to get to know ourselves in the same way.

Imagine you are on your favorite chat show. Begin asking yourself questions like, 'what is your favorite book?' and 'who is the most important person in your life?' then try asking follow-up questions to delve a little deeper, like 'why is that your favorite book?', 'why are they so important to you?' and so on.

Do a ten-minute interview and try to learn something new about yourself. Feel your compassion and understanding towards yourself grow.

Pamper yourself
Positive

After a job well done, or even a job well attempted, it's important to acknowledge your efforts and reward yourself in some way. Write a list of what a reward looks like to you. It might be:

- a yoga class
- a hair cut
- a massage
- watching TV
- a candy bar
-
-
-
-
-
-

Indulge in the above whenever you need to, but especially after you have attempted something out of your comfort zone. It will encourage you to go out there and do your best again and again.

The weight of the labels that we attach to ourselves can become a real burden to drag around.

Take a quiet moment to yourself, away from the usual noise and chatter of your daily life and close your eyes.

Begin to imagine the labels that you have tied to yourself, dangling from your wrists, your ears, your waist, your feet.

REMOVE THE LABELS

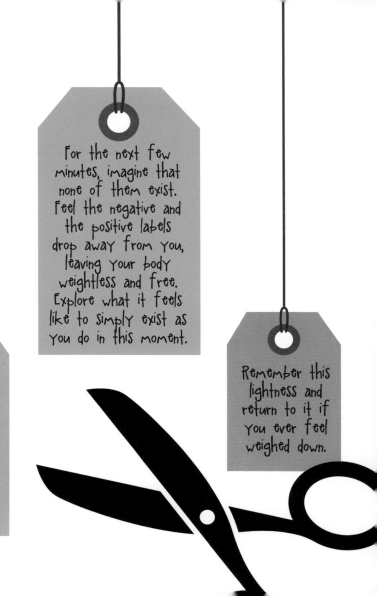

For the next few minutes, imagine that none of them exist. Feel the negative and the positive labels drop away from you, leaving your body weightless and free. Explore what it feels like to simply exist as you do in this moment.

What do these labels say? Are there any that you do not like? What would you prefer them to say?

Remember this lightness and return to it if you ever feel weighed down.

Be
PREPARED,
not SCARED

For those days you dread, write yourself a plan of how you are going to be ready for whatever comes your way. It might include packing snacks, asking for help, wearing your lucky socks, packing an extra pen, or remembering earplugs.

Whatever it is, it doesn't need to be a long list, just a few things or action points that will help jump-start your day with some positive preparation!

FOOD FOR POSITIVE THOUGHT

If you have been STEWing over some negative thoughts and they have become inGRAINed into your diet, then this exercise is for you!

Thoughts can feed our emotions – feeling bad about how you look? Your mind may start unhelpfully listing all the things you like least about your body. Imagine you are making a purely delicious dinner of your thoughts today.

As soon as a bitter thought enters your mind, think 'do I really want to ingest this?' If not, then pick something more positive from your mind's cupboard that will be nourishing and make you feel subLIME! Bon appetit!

ACCEPT YOUR NEEDS

One way to try to feel more positive and accepting about a situation is to identify the need for something within it.

For instance, if you find that you have to go somewhere you don't want to, think, 'I need to go here for X and I accept that.' If you wake up and don't want to go to work, think, 'I need to go to work for X and I accept that.'

Reminding yourself of the motivation behind your actions can give you the positive boost you need to get the job done!

Notes

Use this page to record what works for you, and any other techniques or strategies you might discover.

....

....

....

....

....

....

....

....

....

....

....

....

....

....

....